The Twilight Realm

Ghosts

Please visit our website, **www.garethstevens.com**. For a free color catalog of all our high-quality books, call toll free 1-800-542-2595 or fax 1-877-542-2596.

Library of Congress Cataloging-in-Publication Data

Pipe, Jim, 1966-
 Ghosts / Jim Pipe.
     p. cm. — (The twilight realm)
 Includes bibliographical references (p.   ) and index.
 ISBN 978-1-4339-8752-6 (pbk.)
 ISBN 978-1-4339-8753-3 (6-pack)
 ISBN 978-1-4339-8751-9 (library binding)
 1. Ghosts—Juvenile literature. I. Title.
 BF1461.P5725 2013
 133.1—dc23
                                          2012038518

Published in 2013 by
Gareth Stevens Publishing
111 East 14th Street, Suite 349
New York, NY 10003

© 2013 Gareth Stevens Publishing

Produced for Gareth Stevens by Wayland a division of Hachette Children's Books
a Hachette UK company
www.hachette.co.uk

Editor: Paul Manning
Designer: Paul Manning

Picture Credits
All images © Shutterstock except:

7 (Wem Town Hall), Tony O'Rahilly; 12 (Harry Price), Wikimedia Commons; Harry Price's ghosthunting kit, courtesy Paul Adams; 13, coloured images of Borley Rectory by Steven Wiltshire; 14, 16, 17, 21, 22, 23, Wikimedia Commons; 25, Bill Hind.

Printed in the United States of America

CPSIA compliance information: Batch CW13GS: For further information contact Gareth Stevens, New York, New York at 1-800-542-2595.

The Twilight Realm

Ghosts

Jim Pipe

Gareth Stevens
Publishing

Contents

Spooked!

Do ghosts really exist? Nobody knows for sure. Many people say that they only exist in people's imagination. But others claim that spirits of the dead really can come back to haunt the living.

We use the word "ghost" to describe a whole host of things that we can't explain – a sudden shiver down the spine, a weird smell, a fork that mysteriously flies through the air, or a gruesome face at the window…

Many believe that ghosts are restless souls that cannot find peace in death. Some seek a proper burial, others seek revenge on their killers. Other specters try to warn people of danger. They let people know they're there by moving objects or making noises.

Most of us go through life without ever seeing a ghost. But if you believe the stories, there are malevolent spooks out there that like to play tricks on the living – and some can even do you physical harm.

▲ *Who's that tapping at your window? Is it a ghost, or just a branch blowing in the wind?*

"The chain he drew was clasped about his middle. It was long, and wound about him like a tail… His body was transparent, so that Scrooge, observing him, and looking through his waistcoat, could see the two buttons on his coat behind."

From *A Christmas Carol* by Charles Dickens

Ghostly Forms

In stories, ghosts come in many forms. People describe them as being hazy, shadowy, or like a bright light. In some tales, ghosts try to communicate with the living by whispering or by writing on walls.

In classic hauntings, people describe ghosts appearing in the clothes they wore when they were alive. Some ghosts are headless – a sign that they met a violent death. The spookiest specters have no eyes. When you look at them, two dark sockets gaze back!

Ghosts are often linked to a particular place. Both the Tower of London and the prison island of Alcatraz (off the coast of San Francisco) are said to be haunted by the ghosts of prisoners.

Some spirits are claimed to have a powerful effect on electrical equipment, making batteries go dead or lights go on and off for no reason. One reportedly haunted farmhouse in Wales had a huge electricity bill as a result!

◄ *This photograph was taken when Wem Town Hall in Shropshire, UK, burned to the ground in 1995. At the time, nobody saw this girl standing in the doorway of the burning building. Could she be a ghost captured on film…?*

◄ *…Sadly, no. Ten years later, it was revealed that the photographer had used camera trickery to insert this figure of a young girl standing in a doorway into his pictures of the Wem Town Hall blaze. Who says the camera never lies?*

7

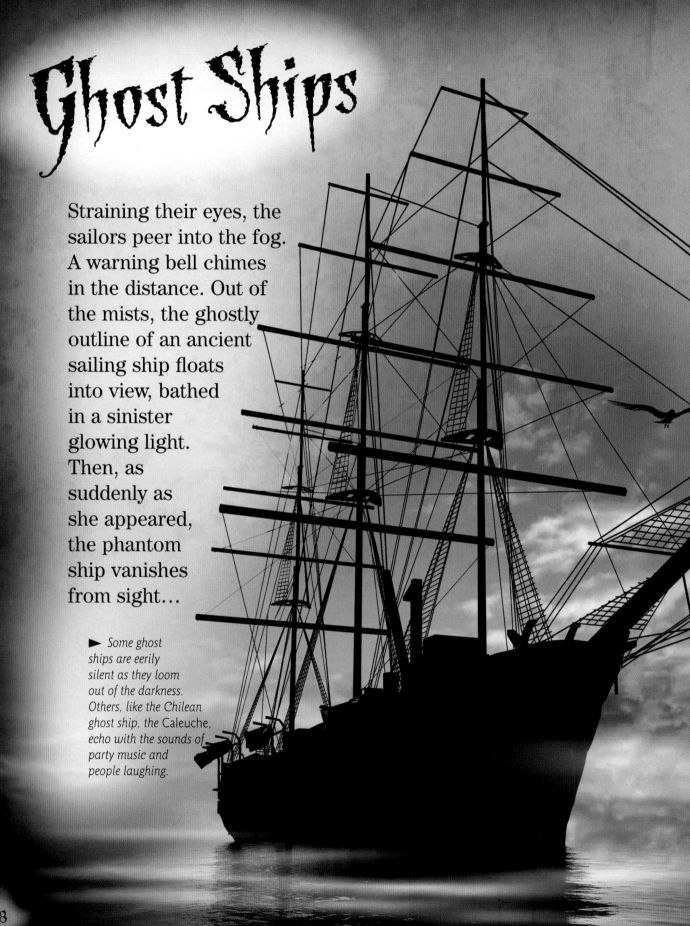

Ghost Ships

Straining their eyes, the sailors peer into the fog. A warning bell chimes in the distance. Out of the mists, the ghostly outline of an ancient sailing ship floats into view, bathed in a sinister glowing light. Then, as suddenly as she appeared, the phantom ship vanishes from sight…

▶ *Some ghost ships are eerily silent as they loom out of the darkness. Others, like the Chilean ghost ship, the* Caleuche, *echo with the sounds of party music and people laughing.*

Phantom ships appear in many a seafarer's tale. Some, like the *Lady Lovibund*, seem so real that other ships have even sent out lifeboats to pick up the crew. In February 1748, the *Lady Lovibund's* captain set sail with his new bride onboard. Unfortunately, his first mate was also madly in love with the same woman. In a jealous rage, the mate deliberately steered the ship onto the deadly Goodwin Sands. The ship sank and all on board were drowned. Every 50 years, so the story goes, the *Lady Lovibund* returns to haunt the waters off the Kent coast. A trick of the light? Possibly. But this doesn't explain the reported sounds of ghostly laughter or creaking ship's timbers – or the sight of a vessel lost at sea two centuries before!

▼ *According to seafaring lore, any ship that encountered the blood-red sails of the* Flying Dutchman *on the high seas was destined for doom and disaster.*

The Flying Dutchman

No ghost ship is more infamous than the *Flying Dutchman*, named after its captain, Hendrik Van der Decken. In 1680, Van der Decken was sailing along the coast of Africa, when his ship was caught in a fierce storm near the Cape of Good Hope.

Maddened by weeks of battling with huge seas, the captain killed the first mate and vowed to sail around the Cape, "even if God would let me sail to Judgement Day!" Despite his efforts, the vessel sank. Van der Decken and his ghost ship were cursed to sail the oceans forevermore, bringing death and destruction to anyone who set eyes on them.

In 1881, the future British king, George V, then serving on the *HMS Bacchante*, recorded in his diary the appearance of "a strange red light as of a phantom ship all aglow." The next day, the crew member who first reported sighting the ship died after falling from the rigging. The young George V was convinced the ship he had seen was the *Flying Dutchman*.

As well as ships, people claim to have seen ghostly planes, trains, and buses. Drivers have even been known to swerve out of the way for phantom horsedrawn coaches. What would YOU do if you saw a ghost ship heading your way?

Are You Being Haunted?

Every ghost has its own way of getting in touch with the living. Some are believed to spook animals such as cats and dogs. The specters that haunt Cothele House in Cornwall, England, are said to fill the rooms with a strong smell of herbs!

▶ *Some ghosts appear one minute and are gone the next. Others gradually fade from view, until only their head or arm is visible.*

Eerie Lights?

Bright, glowing orbs of white or blue light whizzing around or drifting through the air have often been photographed at haunted sites. Sudden flashes of light have also been reported.

Sudden Chills?

A sudden inexplicable chill in the atmosphere is another sign that there may be spooks around. Such "cold spots" have been reported at the Rouse Road Cemetery in Orlando, Florida, said to be haunted by a ghost from the 1800s.

Moans and Groans?

According to the stories, ghosts can create all kinds of weird sounds – including musical ones! Jazz bandleader Glenn Miller died in a plane crash on December 15, 1944. The ghostly sound of a trombone has been heard in the English Channel, near the spot where his plane is thought to have come down.

Objects Moved or Missing?

Some annoying ghosts reportedly move pictures, write on walls, and slam doors. Others like to stack household objects such as chairs or jars on top of one another. Helpful phantoms have also been reported to restart old machines, such as unwound clocks.

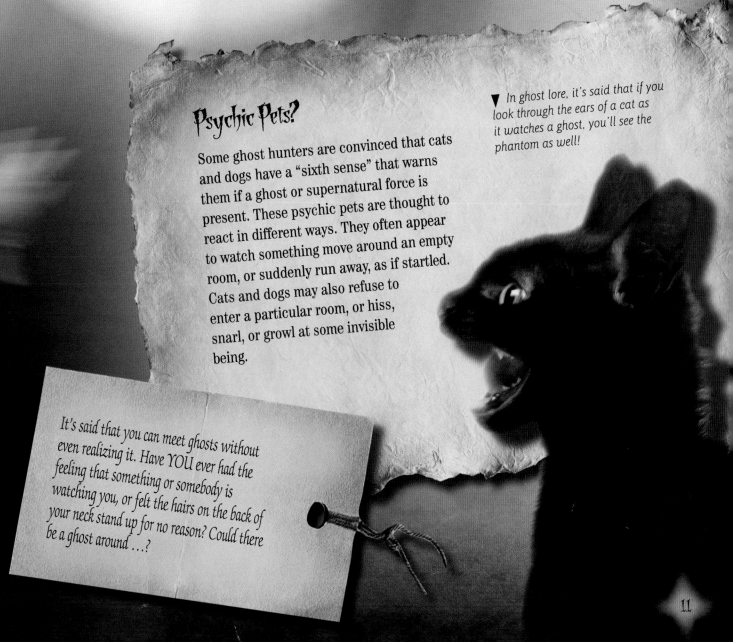

Psychic Pets?

Some ghost hunters are convinced that cats and dogs have a "sixth sense" that warns them if a ghost or supernatural force is present. These psychic pets are thought to react in different ways. They often appear to watch something move around an empty room, or suddenly run away, as if startled. Cats and dogs may also refuse to enter a particular room, or hiss, snarl, or growl at some invisible being.

▼ In ghost lore, it's said that if you look through the ears of a cat as it watches a ghost, you'll see the phantom as well!

It's said that you can meet ghosts without even realizing it. Have YOU ever had the feeling that something or somebody is watching you, or felt the hairs on the back of your neck stand up for no reason? Could there be a ghost around …?

Ghost Hunter...

Phantom footsteps, ringing bells, ghostly chanting, and sightings of a coach driven by two headless coachmen – would YOU want to spend a night in the most haunted house in Britain?

In the 1930s, ghost hunter Harry Price (*right*) and a team of paranormal investigators spent many nights doing just that. The strange events at Borley Rectory in Sussex, England, had driven several of its past owners from the house. One occupant claimed she was awoken by a slap in the face. Another said she woke up to find the gloomy figure of a tall man in a dark hat looming over her bed.

▲ *Harry Price (1881–1948), ghost hunter and pioneer of "psychical research."*

▲ *Borley Rectory, shown here before and after it was destroyed by fire in 1943. During the blaze, it was said that ghostly figures could be seen moving around in the flames.*

... or Ghost Faker?

Price claimed that two spirits haunted Borley Rectory. The first was that of a former nun, Marie Lairre, who had been strangled by her husband in the 1660s. According to Price, Marie was responsible for the desperate pleas for help scrawled on the walls of the house. Another spirit, named Sunex Amures, warned Price that the rectory would burn down and that proof of Marie's murder would be found in the ruins. Soon after, Borley Rectory did burn down, and the bones of a young woman were discovered in the rubble. After the remains were buried, the phantom nun was never seen again.

After Price's death in 1948, other investigators claimed he had faked the evidence. They said that a mysterious "flying brick" photographed on a visit with a reporter had simply been flung by a workman, and that stones that appeared to hurtle inexplicably through the air had in fact been thrown by Price. But ever since the rectory was first built, visitors had reported chilling sights and sounds around the house and grounds. Was Borley Rectory *really* haunted? We will never know!

◄ *Harry Price's "ghost hunter's kit" included a remote-control movie camera, a fingerprinting kit, and portable telephones to keep in touch with members of his team.*

'Robinson [the owner] waited in the dark with a hockey stick and made lunges at "something" that passed him. He never struck anything. Then stones were thrown: small round pebbles hurtled through the air, or came rolling down the stairs.'

Harry Price describing a haunting at Borley

13

Terrors of the Night

Don't believe in ghosts? Then stay away from the terrifying ghost tales of M.R. James. Their message is clear: "Watch out, or this could happen to you…"

Professor Parkins didn't believe in ghosts – and scorned anyone who did. He had planned to spend a few days on his own in a quiet seaside town. When a friend asked him to visit an ancient site down by the beach, Parkins agreed to take a look.

After checking into his room, the professor set off to investigate. Out on the sand dunes, he soon stumbled on a curious metal object shaped like a whistle. Back in his room, he couldn't resist giving it a blow.

All of a sudden, the window was blasted open by a mighty gust of wind. It took all of Parkins' strength to shut it. He thought nothing of it, but that night, he was haunted by disturbing visions of a dark stranger prowling along the beach…

M.R. James (1862-1936) was a well-known scholar who wrote ghost stories for fun. Asked if he really believed in them, he replied, "I am prepared to consider evidence and accept it if it satisfies me."

After breakfast the next day, a young boy ran howling into another guest, Colonel Wilson. He claimed he'd seen a hideous face staring out from Parkins' room! The professor ran upstairs, but found only his clothes in a tangled mess. What was going on?

That night, Parkins was woken by a strange rustling noise. In the dim light, he could see a shadowy figure sitting on the empty bed opposite. The creature stood up and Parkins screamed at the sight of its gruesome face – a mass of crumpled linen. Hearing his wild cries, the colonel burst into the room. The terrible specter leapt out of the window – but the professor had seen enough. He was now a believer…

Christmas Shivers

The story retold here, "Oh, Whistle, and I'll Come to You, My Lad," is one of a famous collection of spine-tingling tales by M.R. James. Many were written for James's Christmas Eve parties, when he loved to give his friends the shivers as he read his tales aloud by candlelight. James's ghosts are mostly evil spirits that appear quietly at first, but eventually terrify their victims out of their wits.

The moral is that messing with old books or objects can summon spirits from beyond the grave. Professor Parkins finds an ancient inscription on the whistle that reads: "Thief – if you blow this whistle you'll be sorry." He ignored the warning and blew it – not once, but twice! You have been warned!

Do any of YOUR family members like to tell ghost stories? Do you swap scary tales with friends sitting round a campfire in the dark? Ask your relatives or teachers – perhaps they remember living near a haunted house when they were younger.

Ghosts on Camera

Photos and videos can provide dramatic evidence of ghosts and spirits. The hard part is proving that they are genuine. In the early 1900s, English photographer William Hope (1863–1933) earned a reputation for capturing the real thing on camera. But was he telling the truth?

◄ *In this photograph by William Hope, a cloaked specter hovers over the shoulder of a couple as they pose for the camera. Spooky – until you know that the "ghost" was a living relative of a member of Hope's spiritualist group!*

Where would YOU go to photograph a ghost? Hanging out in cemeteries with cameras and video recorders will certainly give you goosebumps. But a better bet are old houses where ghostly apparitions have already been spotted.

illiam Hope's interest in the spirit world began in 1905 after he snapped a "ghost" while he and a friend took turns photographing one another. Though trained as a carpenter, Hope soon became known as an expert in ghosts and the paranormal.

After World War I, Hope's "spirit photographs" grew in popularity, as people whose relatives had died in the war searched for a way to get in touch with loved ones. In 1922, ghost hunter Harry Price revealed that Hope was faking his photos. But even after this, many people still believed that his blurry images offered a glimpse into the "spirit world."

▲ *This famous photo taken in 1936 is supposed to show a ghostly "Brown Lady" floating down the stairs of Raynham Hall in Norfolk, England.*

Seeing Double

In Victorian times, "spirit photographers" used a number of tricks to fake their pictures. In those days, you had to sit for about a minute to have your picture taken, so all the photographer's costumed assistant had to do was to sneak into the background for a few seconds to create a shadowy image. Double exposures, made by exposing the same piece of film twice, were another way of making spooky images.

Cameras have come a long way in the last 150 years, but many modern "ghost pictures" still show hazy, blurry shapes, or white blobs called orbs which could easily be caused by scattered light from the camera's flash.

Poltergeist!

A chair tilts before being hurled through the air. A door suddenly slams with a sound like thunder. Could it be a poltergeist, a "noisy spirit" said to light fires and make objects fly around the room? Watch out – poltergeists like to stick close to a particular place or person, often a child or teenager…

▲ Poltergeists are malevolent ghosts that enjoy playing tricks on the living. These invisible houseguests have even been reported to hurl large stones or lift their victims into the air.

Sceptics argue that poltergeist stories are nearly always the result of hoaxing or trickery. But according to believers, angry or restless spirits really can turn people's lives upside down – and the evidence can be compelling. What do YOU think?

In 1977, bizarre things started to happen in the North London home of Peggy Hodgson and her four children. On the night of August 30, the beds in which two of the children were sleeping began to jolt violently up and down. The next night, a heavy chest of drawers started shuffling across the bedroom floor. Loud bangs and knocks went on all night. In the morning, the terrified Hodgson family moved next door to a neighbor's house.

When the police arrived to investigate, one officer saw a chair shoot across the room. Over the next few days, toy blocks and marbles were thrown around the house. For several months, the haunting continued. Fires broke out, then went out on their own. Mysterious puddles appeared on the floor. Eleven-year-old Janet Hodgson was flung out of bed and, on one occasion, was seen by passers-by hovering in midair at an upstairs window. When questioned by a paranormal investigator, Janet replied in a low, gravelly voice from deep in her throat. The voice said it was a man named Bill, who had died in the house some years earlier.

Though Janet later admitted faking some of the events to get attention, most of the paranormal phenomena had no explanation – and the family themselves were clearly scared by them. Most chilling of all, when Bill's son heard tape recordings of the poltergeist "speaking" through Janet, he immediately recognized his father's voice!

▼ *The "Enfield Poltergeist" was covered in many British papers at the time.*

▼ *This photograph of Janet Hodgson apparently flying across the bedroom is one of several taken during the Enfield haunting. Janet said later: "When you're levitated with force and you don't know where you're going to land, it's very frightening. I still don't know how it happened."*

The hous
of strang
happening

Tricks of the Light

Most of us have looked into a cloud and seen a human face, or remembered seeing something that wasn't really there. So can ghosts be explained away as tricks of the light, delusions, or dreams?

Our brains are designed to make sense of the world around us, but they're not infallible. A group of people who witness a shocking murder often remember it very differently. That's because when we get very excited or afraid, our senses often focus on small details rather than on the whole event.

Once an idea gets into our head, it's hard to shake it off. If someone tells us a creepy old building is haunted, we're much more likely to be aware of strange noises or flickering shadows.

▲ Can you see a ghostly face in this swirling smoke? Do you hear strange voices when you run the faucet? Don't worry, it's probably just your senses playing tricks on you!

"We don't believe that ghosts know what time of day it is, so we prefer to go ghost hunting at night. During the day, shadows play tricks, and the light gets refracted [bent] by air heated by the Sun."

Coldwinds Ghost Hunting Society

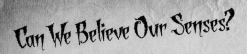

Can We Believe Our Senses?

The human tendency to see shapes and patterns in random objects – like spotting a face in a cloud – is called "pareidolia."

Once you start looking, you can see spooky faces everywhere: in gnarled tree roots, crumpled sheets, rust stains, ink blots, or flickering flames. Our ears play the same trick when we listen to recorded sounds – so that we sometimes hear whispered words when there is really only random noise.

Researchers have found that very deep sounds can be especially disturbing because we *sense* low vibrations without actually being able to hear them. In one experiment, scientists noticed that switching off a fan suddenly made the room feel less haunted, even though the sound made by the fan was too low to be heard by the human ear.

Many of the cold spots linked to hauntings have been explained by drafty windows or chimneys. Our bodies don't always sense where a gust of air is coming from.

◄ *This ghostly "face" was first spotted by Maria Pereira on the floor of her home in southern Spain in the 1970s. Unnerved, Maria had the floor broken up and re-laid – but the face appeared again! After digging down two meters, workmen found an old graveyard. Though the skeletons were removed, the face kept returning. Some claimed the evidence was faked, but "The House of the Faces" soon became a local tourist attraction.*

Raising the Dead

In the days before radio and TV, getting in touch with your dead friends and relatives was a popular way to spend an evening. At special meetings called séances, people known as mediums claimed to be able to use their psychic powers to help people communicate with the spirits of the dead.

Séances usually took place in someone's home. The lights were turned down low, as it was claimed that spirits were easier to see in the dark. Skeptics pointed out that it also made it easier to fool people into believing they had seen or heard a ghost.

A rush of cold air followed by knocking sounds announced that the "spirit" had entered the room. The dead passed on messages by writing in chalk on "spirit slates." Some famous mediums, such as Florence Cook, even claimed they could make ghosts appear and shake hands with, or even hug, the living!

► *This photo of a séance was taken in the 1920s. Notice the hand reaching up from below the table. Could this be a visitor from the spirit world?*

Voices From Beyond

Where did the idea for séances come from? In the mid 19th century, so the story goes, two young sisters, Kate and Maggie Fox, lived in an old farmhouse that was said to be haunted. In March 1848, the Fox family began to be disturbed by strange sounds so loud that the beds shook. Fed up with the noise, Kate is said to have challenged the spirit to imitate her clapping – and was amazed when it clapped back right away!

The sisters worked out a method of communicating with their spirit by asking questions and getting knocks as answers. By November 1849, Kate and Maggie were showing off their skills in public.

Soon, people were flocking to see the Fox sisters. Not everyone believed they were telling the truth. Some newspapers and experts claimed that the sisters faked their results by cracking their ankle joints or using hidden gadgets.

During one test, the girls were tied around the ankles, but still managed to produce eerie rapping sounds. A group of women also checked the girl's clothes to make sure that nothing was hidden there to produce the sounds. Nothing was ever found. In 1888, however, Maggie showed how she pulled off the trick – she could crack her toes so loudly, the sound could even be heard at the back of the theater!

► A Ouija board is marked with numbers and letters. At a séance, the medium supposedly moves his or her finger around the board to spell out messages from the dead.

Do YOU think you've seen a ghost? Was it at night? Remember that it's easy to see strange things in the dark. And tired minds often mix up reality and dreams…

YES
ABCDEFGHIJKLM
1234567890
NOPQRSTUVWXY
HELLO
Magical Talking Board
GOOD BYE

Ghost Watch

Ghost hunting may seem like a piece of cake: just stake out a haunted house and wait for your phantom to appear. But it's full of surprises. People describe hours of boredom, then a moment of pure terror as an invisible force knocks them right off their feet!

▲ *Deserted buildings often seem haunted just because no one lives in them. Water running below a house can cause creaks and groans. At night, houses cool down, making the walls produce odd noises.*

Early ghost hunters used candles to pick up ghostly breezes. They sprinkled flour on surfaces to pick up ghostly prints. Today's ghost detectives use hi-tech equipment as well as notebooks and pens to take notes. Motion detectors and sensors are linked to laptop computers and automatic cameras to catch ghosts on video. Sounds are recorded digitally with highly sensitive microphones.

An electromagnetic field detector, or EMD, is a favorite device. It locates and tracks energy sources, and some ghost hunters believe a spike in energy is a sign that a ghost is present. Sensitive thermometers pick up sudden changes in temperature, which can help to confirm cold spots. Serious ghost hunters work in groups, so there's always someone else around to confirm a sighting.

Where to Look

Creepy old mansions and castles are obvious places to look for ghosts. But any spot where people have lived or worked can be haunted. Ghosts can appear at any time, and most sightings are in daylight hours. Certain places seem to attract ghosts, such as the town of Atchison, in Kansas, or the Tower of London, home to the ghost of Anne Boleyn, who was beheaded there in 1536.

Unlikely places can turn out to be haunted. In 2011, construction work at one of England's largest theme parks came to a halt after workmen reported that a headless monk was haunting the site of a new waterslide at Thorpe Park, just outside London. Ghost hunters later discovered the new ride was being built over an ancient burial ground!

▼ Churches and abbeys are often said to be haunted. This churchyard in Prestbury, Gloucestershire, is claimed to be one of the most haunted places in England.

The Vanishing Hitchhiker

Some of the best known ghost stories aren't written down. They're passed around by word of mouth until they become urban legends. One of the scariest is the tale of the vanishing hitchhiker…

A teenage girl and her friend are driving down a lonely country road on their way to a local dance. Suddenly, a good-looking boy appears in the headlights, standing at the side of the road and thumbing a ride. The girls hit the brakes and offer him a lift. The boy asks to be taken home, but they persuade him to come along to the dance instead.

▼ In some versions of the story, the mysterious traveler vanishes into thin air while the car that picked him or her up is still moving!

The boy climbs into the back seat. Even though it's a warm night, he's shivering with cold, so one of the girls lends him her jacket. The three teenagers dance through the night, but as morning approaches, the boy asks for a lift home. After the girls drop him off, one of them remembers that the boy still has her jacket. Never mind. It's a good excuse to see him again the next day!

But the next day when the girls return to the boy's house, they find only an elderly woman living there. She explains that her son died years ago in a car accident. She points down the road to the cemetery where he's buried. Privately deciding the old lady is crazy, the girls head off to the cemetery. There, they find the jacket draped over a grave. Written on the tombstone is the boy's name and the date of his death – exactly twelve years earlier…

"I Believe in Mary Worth..."

Mirrors crop up in many hair-raising ghost stories, like the tale of Mary Worth. Many years ago, this beautiful young girl was so badly scarred in an accident that nobody could look at her. Fearing she would go mad if she ever saw herself again, her mother hid all the mirrors in the house. But one night Mary crept into her mother's room and stole her mirror. Seeing her own hideous face, Mary screamed and sobbed, putting a terrible curse on anyone who thought of her when they gazed at themselves in a mirror.

According to the urban legend, if you stand in front of a mirror and say "Mary Worth, Mary Worth, I believe in Mary Worth," you'll be cursed too. One group of girls who tried it turned out the lights first. After a while they saw a green glow in the mirror. Slowly the ghostly face of Mary Worth appeared. Then, one of the girls let out a horrible scream. When they turned on the lights, she had deep scratches down her cheek!

Can YOU think up an urban legend to scare your friends? Look around your area for a spooky old house in which to set your story. If you need a character, try delving into your local history. Are there any tales of people who died long ago under mysterious circumstances?

Twilight Quiz

1. While exploring a haunted house, you feel a sudden cold spot. Should you:

   a Say loudly: "Come on, show me that spooky stuff! The ghostbusters are here!"?

   b Eliminate natural explanations like drafty windows or chimneys? If none exists, mark the spot clearly on your plan of the building.

   c Put on a warm coat and find somewhere a bit more cozy to do your ghost hunting?

2. You're asked to investigate a house with a suspected poltergeist. Should you:

   a Demolish the house to see if it's built on an ancient grave site?

   b Find out the history of the building, then carefully interview all the inhabitants to find out if it's a hoax?

   c Refuse to enter the house without a helmet and padded jacket just in case there's any violent plate-throwing?

3. You want to catch a ghost on camera. What's the best way of doing it?

   a Put the biggest flash you can on your camera. Hopefully, the bright light will stun the ghost long enough to catch it on film.

   b Pick a spot where spooky activity has been confirmed. Make sure all your equipment is working and bring extra batteries in case the ghosts make them go dead.

   c Set up all your automatic sensors and cameras and go home for the night. After a sound night's sleep, you can check all the gear in the morning.

4. At a séance, the medium tells you that a spirit has entered the room. Should you:

   a Ask, "Do you ever get bored, and what's the food like where you are?"

   b Keep an open mind, but make sure the medium isn't trying to trick you?

   c Ask if you can go to the restroom, as all this talk of ghosts is making you nervous?

5. You're face to face with what can only be described as a ghost. What next?

   a Scream "BOO!" as loudly as you can and wave your arms wildly. That'll show the phantom who's boss!

   b Stay calm. Watch the specter for a minute or two, then ask quietly who they are. Try to remember everything you see and hear.

   c You've spotted your ghost, so the job is done. Get out of there as fast as your legs will carry you.

CHECK YOUR SCORE

Mostly 'a's You've certainly got guts, but you'd probably scare the ghosts off!

Mostly 'b's Perfect. You're cool-headed, brave, and sensible. We'll be in touch soon!

Mostly 'c's This job might not be for you. Sounds like you'd be spooked by a creaking door.

Glossary

apparition the visible appearance of a ghost

Beyond, the a phrase to describe the "spirit world," where people's souls are believed to live after death; see **spiritualism**

cemetery a place where dead people are buried

delusion seeing, or believing in, something that does not really exist

draft a current of cold air

exposure when light reacts with photographic film or paper

flash a burst of light produced by a camera that lets you take photographs in the dark

gadget a useful device or piece of equipment

gnarled twisted, misshapen

gruesome horrible or revolting

herb a type of plant used to add flavor to food

inscription words written or carved on an object

malevolent wicked, wishing to harm people

medium a person who claims to use "psychic" powers to communicate with the dead

motion detector an electronic device that measures movement

orb a ball of white light, claimed by some people to be evidence of paranormal activity

Ouija board a board with letters on it, used by people at a séance

paranormal unable to be explained scientifically

pareidolia name given to the way we tend to see human faces in random patterns

phantom a person or thing that does not really exist

poltergeist a "noisy ghost" that can be heard but not seen, and is claimed to be able to make objects move and fly through the air

portable able to be carried around

psychic belonging to the world of the mind, soul, or spirit

rectory a house lived in by a priest or vicar

refract to change the direction of a beam of light

Glossary (continued)

rigging the ropes that support a ship's mast and sails

scarred permanently and visibly marked by an unpleasant experience

scholar someone who has made a special study of a particular subject

scorn to view something or someone as being silly or stupid

séance a meeting where people try to communicate with the spirits of the dead

sensor a device which detects and measures a physical property such as heat, light, or movement

skeptic someone who questions beliefs or opinions held by other people

specter a ghost or phantom

spike a sudden increase or rise in something

spiritualism the belief that the souls of dead people continue to exist in a world of the spirit

trombone a musical instrument made of brass

unnerved frightened, scared

urban legend a well-known story that has been passed around by word of mouth

waistcoat a sleeveless jacket buttoned at the front

Further Reading and Websites

Further Reading

Ghosts and Other Spectres, Anita Ganeri (Dark Side series, Wayland)

Ghost Files: The Haunting Truth, The Ghost Society (Harper Collins)

The Other Side: A Teen's Guide to Ghost Hunting and the Paranormal, Marley Gibson (Graphia Books)

Encyclopedia Horrifica: The Terrifying TRUTH! About Vampires, Ghosts, Monsters and More, Joshua Gee (Scholastic Books)

The Unexplained: Encounters with Ghosts, Monsters and Aliens, Jim Pipe (Ticktock Media Ltd.)

The Best Ghost Stories Ever, Christopher Krovatin (Editor) (Scholastic Paperbacks)

Websites

www.ghostsandstories.com
Spooky stories to keep you awake at night!

www.ghostresearch.org/ghostpics
Phantom photographs: are they real or fake? You decide.

www.hauntedhouse.com
A great place to find out if there's a haunted house near you!

http://www.ghoststudy.com/
This website includes tips for would-be ghost hunters.

http://sd4kids.skepdic.com/ghosts.html/
An explanation of what scientists say about ghosts and hauntings.

http://www.skeptiseum.org/index.php?id=none&cat=ghosts
A museum on the web with pictures and descriptions of things from around the world that are connected to a belief in ghosts.

Index